STRATEGIC PLANNING FOR INDEPENDENT SCHOOLS

SUSAN C. STONE

D1598601

National Association of Independent Schools
18 Tremont Street
Boston, Massachusetts 02108

Contents

Contents

Introduction

The Commission on Educational Issues of the National Association of Independent Schools presented a seminar on long-range planning in the summer of 1978. Its purpose was to teach a specific process of long-range planning and policy development for independent schools that had been developed by the commission's staff. NAIS then published a manual entitled *Long-Range Planning for Independent Schools,* written by William D. Berkeley, Jerry Foster, and Richard Zajchowski, the developers of the process and presenters of the seminar. The present book, based on the work of the Commission on Educational Issues, represents additional work on the part of many more people in the independent school community, particularly John A. Bird and Jerry F. Millhon.

An elder statesman once remarked, "If we required people to practice what they preached, we would miss out on a lot of good preaching." This book does not just "preach"; it has grown out of years of working directly with schools, other nonprofit organizations, and commercial entities in strategic planning. It also incorporates experience gained from schools that have attended NAIS planning workshops and put the process into effect. The book is intended to serve as a manual for schools undertaking strategic planning for the first time, schools seeking a method different from one they have already used, or schools looking for a way to revitalize a flagging process. Most of the book is devoted to describing the process of strategic long-range planning and telling how to plan and get it under way in a school. Its main purpose is to aid schools that recognize the need to plan for the future.

Susan Stone
Fall 1986

1
The Case for
Strategic Planning

The NAIS *Trustee Handbook* states that one of the duties of independent school trustees is to "hold in trust the school's future as well as its present." That is an enormous task in a period when change seems to be the only constant, when the rate of change is faster, the magnitude of change is broader, and the quality of change is different from any time in the past.

Turbulence and change, the hallmarks of contemporary society, are harbingers of uncertainty. Peter Drucker writes, in *Managing in Turbulent Times,* "The first task of management is to make sure of the institution's capacity for survival. . . .and to avail itself of new opportunities." He discusses the inadequacies of planning techniques from World War II to the present, which, as a rule, start with what happened yesterday and project that into the future. Drucker concludes that future events cannot be planned but can be foreseen, requiring "strategies for tomorrow, strategies that anticipate where the greatest changes are likely to occur and what they are likely to be, strategies that enable a business—or a hospital, a school, a university—to take advantage of new realities and to convert turbulence into opportunity." Not only success, but survival, mandates that an organization take the long view.

John Greeve, headmaster of Wells School in Richard Hawley's novel, *The Headmaster's Papers,* writes in a letter to his board president, "What an anomaly, an absurdity, to 'plan' a future." After listing items for which the board might raise money, including faculty salaries, financial aid, more library books, and maintenance and expansion of facilities, he continues by saying, "Our predecessors managed to build up quite a coherent and effective Wells without, to my knowledge, the aid of a formal plan."

Mr. Greeve's point of view is no doubt shared by others, and may have been true for many schools, but the point of long-range planning may well be to preserve, not to change, what a school has been. This may mean that a school will have to alter some of the strategies it has long employed in order to stay as it is. Management techniques that served a school well in the past may not work in the future. We have no assurances, in a time of change and discontinuity, that what has been will necessarily continue to be.

Why plan?

Why should a school undertake any kind of planning effort, particularly if it is operating in the black, its enrollment is strong, its endowment is securely invested and managed, and its students and their parents are happy with its program?

Often the only emphasis on planning within a school is the annual budget, an occasional three- to five-year financial forecast, plans for a capital campaign, next year's educational program, or yearly charges to committees. But to make significant change in faculty compensation, professional development, size and composition of the student body, facilities, or sources of income takes a comprehensive plan covering a period of years.

Education in the United States is under the spotlight of the national government, the news media, state legislatures, and almost all the other people who have been to school and thus consider themselves qualified educational experts. One outgrowth has been numerous studies of what works in schools, research on teaching and learning styles, and new insights into the function of the brain. Mix this information with issues such as changing family structures and social values, an unsettled economy, shifts in demographics—particularly among the school-age population—advances in all areas of technology, retraining for multicareer lives, and the shifting profile of who is and who will be teaching in independent schools, and the results are potentially volatile. Considering that any one of these factors could be a catalyst for change, can independent schools afford not to plan ahead?

"Strategic planning"

Schools generally use the term "long-range planning" to characterize the kind of planning they do in conjunction with annual budgeting or when new facilities are needed. "Long-range planning" can also refer to a standing committee of the board that either does not meet very often or has met forever. "Long range" means five years to some people, a year to others, and six months to still others.

The term "strategic planning" has generally replaced "long-range planning." The word "strategy," with its military connotations, implies recognition of an existing situation, a future situation, and some kind of adaptation. Many professional planners see a distinction between strategy and planning: strategy deals with change, whereas planning is operational. Good planning depends on good strategy, which directs and defines the plan.

Strategic planning does not forecast the future. It does raise compelling questions and attempts to fit these questions into a framework from which logical action congruent with the school's mission can follow. In some cases, a change in the mission itself is an obvious or inescapable conclusion.

Most recognized planning processes revolve around a data base and financial forecasting. The process described here does not focus primarily on financial or other data in its beginning phases; numbers come into play largely in the implementation phase. Only after overall direction and goals are determined are price tags put on proposed buildings or programs, "what ifs" in salary administration projected, or specific goals for an endowment campaign set. Because the planning team must make recommendations for the board's approval, it should not spend time developing detailed statistical or financial information before knowing what is wanted or needed. In other words, this process makes the planning team agree on a vision for the school before it decides on specific strategies for attaining that vision, including how to pay for it. The process helps the team to avoid being constrained from the outset by what a school has done or been able to do in the past.

A good planning process produces goals, objectives, and strategies that are consistent with the school's mission statement. It provides for continuous monitoring of external and internal environments, it becomes part of budgeting and financial planning, and it requires consistent, continuous appraisal and revision as needed. It becomes an integral part of the school.

The planning process

Planning allows the school to respond to change, not resist it. In planning that is conducted primarily by a consulting firm or a business school blueprint, recommendations and conclusions are often made by people other than the school's key decision makers, which necessitates ponderous documentation. In a process that includes chief decision makers at every step, on the other hand, the resulting plan can be based on logic rather than on analysis that paralyzes even the most assiduous reader. Research and analysis do have a place in illuminating the rationale of a plan, but schools must balance their desire for data with their resources.

Besides, most of the data needed for planning are already available within the school.

The strategic planning and policy development process described here is quite simple. It begins with careful organization to ensure orderly progression: format and timetable, composition of the planning team, data to be assembled for the team's use. The process continues by concentrating the team's attention on external and internal issues before it begins to develop consensus on the mission and general goals of the school for the future.

The process leads to a two-part result: the *strategic plan,* a conceptual report to the school's board recommending a series of goals for policy, which provides the basis for the *operating plan,* sometimes also called an action or implementation plan.

The process is much like strategic planning for other kinds of organizations, except that it takes into account the nature of an independent school. It focuses widely on trends for the future as well as on what has happened in the past and what is happening now. It identifies why a school exists, the school's long-term vision, and the possible means for achieving that vision. An outline and diagram of the process are given in Appendix B.

Strategic planning and policy development are systematic, yet they rely on creativity and imagination. The process directs the planning team to look outside the school to consider broad trends for the future before turning inward. It encourages the team to explore a range of possible alternatives before narrowing to specific goals and asks the team to be open-minded, and not to be defensive or justify present methods of operation. While the process does not rely solely on numbers, it does call for relevant data and critical measures of financial health that will lead to practical implementation plans. It also works well for the self-assessment that is part of accreditation. Most important, the process can be tailored to the needs of an individual school.

The process involves members of all parts of the school's community. At the same time, it respects the separate responsibilities of the administration — particularly the head — and the board for operations and policy making, respectively.

The importance of selecting people carefully for the planning team cannot be overstated. Involving people from all segments of the school's community is vital; planning that is top-down or bottom-up rarely succeeds because not enough people feel committed.

Another critical point is how well the team itself functions, for only if the final report reflects consensus can the plan be carried out with the commitment required to see it through.

And, though long-range planning does not always mean massive fund raising and radical change, it usually does mean that at least some things will be different. Research shows that even strongly desired change elicits negative reaction at certain points. Here again, a carefully assembled planning team can form the foundation for positive later action.

Flexibility is another key ingredient of the process, which should be adapted to meet the needs of each school. No matter whether it is accomplished in several intensive sessions over a period of months, in one marathon weekend, or during the better part of a school year, the process should have integrity. In addition to the options given here, schools will find still other ways to respond to specific situations. The only immutable rule is that, because each phase builds on the preceding one, each phase is of value and none should be circumvented.

The purpose of strategic planning and policy development, therefore, is to reach agreement on a long-term vision for the school and then work back from that vision to decide what must be done next week, next month, next year toward making that vision reality. This process raises some questions that cannot be answered immediately. The plan set forth here offers a framework within which schools may address questions and issues systematically and make decisions based on long-term considerations. The plan functions as an internal guide that allows the school to look forward in the face of a changing world.

2
Getting Started

Successful planning depends directly on how carefully the preliminary stages are thought out. Decisions that must be made early are the composition and leadership of the planning team, an overall timetable for completion of the work, what background information the team will need and who is to procure it, and general logistical support for the planning effort.

The head of the school must want to initiate the planning process and take part in it. The head's role during much of the process is that of a participant. As the planning process moves into the report-drafting phase and on into implementation, the head becomes more and more visible. The head must be open and objective throughout. Enthusiasm on the part of the leader of the school can inspire other team members; negative comments and reactions can intimidate them or discount their contributions to the effort.

When it is time to compile a report, the head should take the leading role as author or retain control if someone else is delegated to do the actual writing. No other member of the planning team has a better overview of the school; the results of the plan are likely to affect the head more than anyone else in the school; and it is the head, as chief administrator and professional leader of the school, who will be charged with primary responsibility for carrying out the plan.

The planning team

The right size for a planning team varies from school to school, but having anywhere from twelve to twenty usually allows all parts of the school community to be represented. Fewer than twelve is usually too small to involve everyone and build momentum for eventual acceptance of a plan; more than twenty tends to be unwieldy.

If a choice can be made, it is better to err on the side of inclusiveness. If adding several more people will move the plan ahead, then it is a good idea to do so. But time may militate against choosing the larger number, for the longer the time, the harder it is to keep a large number of people involved. In general, the smaller the group, the more personally involved team members are and the more they understand and appreciate their role in the process.

Who should serve?

Candidates for the planning team should come from the largest possible cross section of the school—administrators, faculty members, parents, students, graduates, and trustees. The exact representation of each category will vary from school to school, and some people will represent more than one constituency. Because the success of the planning effort rests directly on the quality and composition of the team, the aim should be to achieve a broad range of experience, expertise, and perspective. The rapport and camaraderie that develop within the team can serve the school for months and years to come.

Administrators most often designated for team membership, along with the head of the school, are division heads, business managers, and development officers.

Faculty members form the heart of the institution and as such should be well represented on the planning team. After all, they, together with members from the administration, will be responsible for carrying out much of the plan.

Parents who are not members of the board of trustees have yet another point of view that is fundamental to effective planning. Parents' association members who know the school well are logical choices for the planning team.

Students are most often overlooked in the planning process. In some schools, it may not seem a good idea to include students because of their age or the timing of the planning process. Other schools may feel that the number of spaces on the team are so few that they should be filled by adults. If students cannot be named as actual members of the planning team, they can be involved in other ways. Special student council activities, creative writing projects, and discussion groups are just a few ways to evoke student ideas.

Graduates of the school can provide critical insight, especially if significant change is contemplated. Graduates seem to be extraordinarily important in the structure of some schools, virtually ignored in others. Planning can give the school an excellent opportunity to involve graduates in new and important ways.

The chairman of the *board of trustees* may or may not be part of the formal planning team. In most schools, it is advisable for that person to serve; if attendance at all meetings or being a formal part of the team is impossible, then keeping the chairman apprised at each step is critical. If the chairman cannot participate, then the chairman-elect is an obvious choice. Other board members designated for service on the team should represent a variety of committee assignments, years on the board, professions, and points of view. Board members should be chosen carefully, for it is they who will be enlisting formal board support.

Another voice that might be added is that of people representing *the wider community* who have no direct link with the school. The leader of a neighboring educational institution, a key member of the chamber of commerce, or an influential member of the business community are some possibilities. Such people need a thorough briefing about the mission and activities of the school and must see some reason to commit time to the effort as members of the planning team.

Criteria for choosing team members, whatever their role, are their ability to attend scheduled meetings, ability to work within a group, ability to work within a disciplined process, and having the respect of colleagues, imagination and creativity, and concern for the future of the school.

Team leadership
Both the trustees and the school's management must be strongly committed to strategic planning; the planning team's leadership should mirror that commitment. The team can be well led by two people—one from the board, the other from the administration or the faculty.

The primary tasks of the team's leaders are to work with the head and board chairman in setting up the team and its timetable, orienting team members, coordinating data and background material, and serving as an internal and external communications link.

The trustee co-leader should be a strong, skilled person who understands the planning process and has the time to devote to this work. He or she should be perceived as having influence within the board and thus major responsibility for "selling" the process and its result to the board.

The faculty or administrator co-leader should have similar personal and leadership qualities and also understand the process.

The respect of colleagues is essential, for this person serves as liaison to both the faculty and the administration.

Team duties

The primary role of the planning team is to develop broad recommendations for future strategy, in the form of policy goals that support the mission of the school, for approval by the board of trustees. These goals precede and give definition to the implementation or strategy developed subsequently by the head, the chairman of the board, and a wide array of people throughout the school community who may or may not have been on the planning team itself. The original task of the team as such is completed when the board approves the preliminary report of its recommendations.

Timetable

The three basic approaches to planning are *the fast track*—working through the process intensively within a few months; *the flexible timetable*—extending the process over several months; and *a school year*—taking most of a school year to complete the process. More than one kind of timetable is possible; examples of timetables and work schedules are given in Appendix C. Whichever timetable is chosen, maintaining momentum is essential.

Fast track

If using the "fast track" approach, the team dedicates approximately two and a half days, preferably in a retreat setting, starting with orientation and moving on to consider external and internal climates, define the school in the future, appraise the school's mission statement, and identify policy goals.

The next steps—preparing and presenting a report—take place

later. Depending on the timetable, the process can be completed in as little as two to three months. (Some schools may make an even shorter schedule, but this is recommended only in unusual circumstances.) After the board approves the conceptual plan, implementation can begin at the discretion of the head and board chairman.

The advantage of the fast track is that it takes less time and energy and maintains momentum and enthusiasm. It is often the only way some schools can get the commitment they need from planning team members. To be successful, however, this approach requires careful advance planning and very skilled, task-oriented leadership and procedures.

Flexible timetable

With a flexible timetable, the same steps as those outlined above are taken, but in four to six sessions, and at intervals of several weeks. The process begins, if possible, with a short retreat and continues over as many months—three to six—as the team leaders deem necessary. Once again, after board approval, formal implementation is begun and completed according to the plan deemed most advantageous by the head and board chairman.

One advantage of this more flexible approach is that it allows more time between sessions for reflection and data gathering. It works well in schools where an extended retreat is not realistic and where team members can commit themselves to a greater number of meetings over a longer period of time.

School year

By using most of a school year, more meetings of shorter duration may be scheduled. An extension of the flexible timetable approach, the school-year format has its same general advantages and works well in a school that has a tradition of very careful, deliberate discussion and no need to meet a more immediate deadline.

Logistics

If the school decides that a retreat is the best way to begin the planning process, the site chosen should be conducive to work as well as relaxation so that the head and other school people can participate fully by being away from the school. Because the planning team needs logistical support from the school—meeting facilities, secretarial services, supplies and mailing facilities, and data from the business and admission offices—it needs to establish a budget for the planning process.

The planning team needs up-to-date information before it can get under way. The data it needs may include

Mission and philosophy statement(s)

Previous planning reports

Budget (in major categories)

Tuition scale

Salary ranges

Size of faculty

Faculty/student ratio and student contact hours

Student financial aid

Size and nature of applicant pool

Number of students accepted, enrolled

Profile of most recent graduating class at admission, at graduation

Immediate plans of most recent graduating class

Comparative figures for the year or years immediately preceding

Information about the surrounding community, also important, might include demographic data, economic indicators, and city and regional planning documents. This kind of information is usually available through the chamber of commerce, local government planning units, and social service agencies.

The school's business office can be of enormous help by using the computer to present financial data in spreadsheet form and to organize other data in graphs and charts.

Background reading about present and future trends helps set the stage and stimulate ideas. Well-chosen articles from the material that abounds on predictions, warnings, trends in education, social values, and national demographics can provide some common vocabulary for team members. The bibliography in Appendix A gives some suggestions.

The team leaders, in collaboration with the head, need to decide what, how much, and when information should be given to the team. The point is to assemble enough data so that the team feels prepared for its task, but not to overwhelm team members with information they neither want nor need or to swamp the business and admission offices with requests. The primary focus of the process is not numbers; at this stage, the team should receive only supporting information, which should be concise and succinct. Whatever additional data the team wants can be generated as needed.

It is necessary to recognize the difference between background data and information that is more appropriately part of the implementation phase. If the team decides, for example, that extensive market research should be undertaken, such research is really part of the later strategy that relates to long-term marketing and public relations goals. Similarly, questionnaires can pinpoint attitudes and opinions if done as part of an integrated plan (unless, of course, majority responses to a questionnaire are intended to replace strategic planning). In other words, opinion surveys and other market research tools are better used as part of a systematic implementation plan after overall goals have been affirmed than they are as techniques for gathering preliminary background information.

Thorough orientation of planning team members completes the groundwork phase. Orientation works best if it can be scheduled before the process actually begins so that everyone involved may learn what is contemplated and how it will be executed and be able to ask questions. Here are points that need to be covered in orientation.

> Names of team members
>
> Nature and duration of the commitment for team members
>
> General calendar outlining each phase and culminating in report to the board (see Appendix C)
>
> Specific calendar giving dates, times, and places for scheduled sessions
>
> Written outline accompanied by description and discussion of the strategic planning and policy development process (see Appendix B)
>
> Background information for the planning team

With the planning team in place, the format designed and scheduled, and orientation completed, the background work is done. The team is ready to proceed.

3
Strategic Planning

The strategic planning phase of the long-range planning process is composed of the following steps.

Considering the external climate
Considering the internal climate
Defining the school in the future
Identifying policy goals
Appraising the school's mission statement
Preparing and presenting a report

The object in this phase is to start by looking beyond the school at issues and trends that may affect it over a period of time, then to look inward at the school itself. After hearing colleagues' interests and concerns, individual team members should be asked to tell what they would like the school to be in the future. These individual "scenarios" are the basis for discussion, consensus, and synthesis; their central themes form goals for future policy. Then, after re-examining the school's mission statement, the planning team can decide whether it is in harmony with the future goals or whether the mission statement needs to be revised. This work is summarized in a report to the board of trustees.

Brainstorming

Team building and consensus are central to the strategic planning process. Brainstorming is a technique well suited to producing a wide range of ideas and to developing a cohesive team. The atmosphere throughout the planning effort should be one of openness and objectivity that is established in large part by the team itself.

Brainstorming contributes to such an atmosphere and encourages the "willing suspension of disbelief" needed for team members to entertain options. It enables all members to participate and promotes collaboration among people who do not often work together. Too often people's participation in a group is limited because they are afraid of being wrong or of appearing foolish. Brainstorming, by its very nature, is nonjudgmental and helps overcome these obstacles.

The tools used for brainstorming sessions are simple.

> An easel or flipchart
> Several pads of newsprint (the 24″ x 36″ size works best)
> Felt-tip markers in vivid colors—a different color for each topic or heading
> Tape that will not injure painted walls
> Walls on which the newsprint may be taped

The rules for brainstorming are equally simple.

> All ideas should be shared, regardless of their seeming whimsicality or relative unimportance
> Evaluation, criticism, and discussion are not allowed
> Ideas should be brief and concise, expressed in few words
> Repetition and "piggybacking" are acceptable

Team leaders must exercise skill in keeping the pace rapid,

enforcing the rules, and preventing any one or two people from dominating. Discussion or evaluation of any kind can cause the group to bog down irretrievably or have the net effect of discounting individual members' contributions. The purpose is to generate a long list of ideas in each category being addressed, not to discuss each item. It is common for teams to list page after page of issues, limited only by the time allotted.

The team leaders may wish to act also as recorders, or to trade that role among team members, writing on the newsprint sheets exactly what each participant says. As each sheet is filled — about ten items per page — it is taped to the wall, thus serving as the group record. After brainstorming sessions are complete, the contents of the newsprint sheets are typed and copies of the lists are sent to each participant. This frees everyone from having to take notes.

Brainstorming sessions are useful not only in creating lists of topics to attune members to future trends and challenges and to their colleagues' interests; they also help to forge team cohesiveness and provide the basis for subsequent steps. Members should review the lists periodically to ensure that the team is continuing to deal with major themes articulated at the beginning. A review of the original lists also helps in evaluating the overall implementation plan that is developed in accordance with the team's final recommendations.

Now for some background on each of the six steps in the strategic planning phase.

External climate

It is difficult, if not impossible, to separate a school from the climate in which it exists. Because context is so vital to effective planning, the process should begin by directing the team's attention to international and national trends that will shape the future and, therefore, affect the school. It has been said that the trouble with living in our time is that "the future just isn't what it used to be"—a good reason why the team should start by looking at issues that seem remote from the school and beginning to look at the school as it might be in the future.

Some current examples of trends that will affect schools in the future are the impact of global thinking and global economics on the curriculum, implications for the classroom of rapidly advancing technology, the tax status of charitable giving, and the effects of changing family structures and social values. The unprecedented numbers of women entering the work force in the fairly recent past has had an enormous impact on schools in terms of the needs of families in which both parents work, their ability to afford independent schooling, before- and after-school child care, limited time for volunteering, and career opportunities for women beyond the traditional few, of which one was teaching. Much of this seems to have come as a surprise to educational institutions used to assessing the impact only of educational issues.

Therefore, looking outside before looking inside provides a non-threatening way to begin strategic planning and alerts the school to external events that can have a profound effect over time.

International and national issues may be grouped in the following general categories: economic, political, social, environmental, technical, demographic, and educational.

The next step is to repeat brainstorming for local issues—those having to do with the region, state, county, or city. These issues are still external, but closer to home. Examples might be the relative economic health of the region, fluctuations in population, the impact of state education reform, the condition and image of the local public schools, city and county planning, the unique nature of the locale, and cultural advantages and disadvantages. Many topics may overlap with those in the international and national lists; it is important to repeat them wherever they apply to the local scene.

It is useful to spend some time brainstorming responses that the school might make to some of the themes that recur. In reviewing the lists, team leaders will be able to discern topics that could be clustered under one larger statement. For instance, if several ideas center on local independent schools as they relate to the public schools, it would be worthwhile to ask for brainstormed responses on that issue. Or if a number of ideas indicate a potential boom in local industry, or concern over major demographic changes, these also would be topics for responses.

Not every local issue listed needs to be responded to—only those that appear to have potential significant impact. Reminding the team that it should keep thinking in terms of issues external to the school helps keep the brainstorming on track.

Issues may be seen as threats or opportunities or both. Team members should be asked to think the unthinkable, to play with a range of possibilities, with no commitment at this stage. Responses should begin with verbs, briefly describing actions the school could take to minimize threats and make the most of opportunities. For instance, if an industrial boom is in the offing, the school's responses might be to make admission information available to local realtors, to work with the chamber of commerce to make presentations to corporations considering relocation in the community, to approach corporate and individual newcomers for various kinds of support. If the issue is competition with local public or private schools, the school might use several strategies to project its image: collaborate in special programs, differentiate its program from those of others, actively recruit students. The team is not being asked at this point to say what the school *should* do, but what it *might* do in response to emerging local trends.

It is a good idea to give typewritten brainstorming lists to team members as soon as possible after each session so that they may refer to them before proceeding. (Additional examples of brainstorming issues are given in Appendix D. Suggestions for the amount of time to allot to different brainstorming activities are given in Appendix C. In using the fast-track approach, typing all the newsprint the team has filled is done only after the retreat is over.)

This planning process can be viewed as a funnel. Brainstorming produces the widest possible range of ideas at the top; these are combined and filtered to identify those ideas that are most appropriate for further discussion and development. (See the diagram in Appendix B.)

Internal climate

Most team members are eager to reach the second stage, talking about internal climate, because it appears to have the most direct relevance to the school. Even so, the leaders should restrain the team until they are satisfied that the preceding steps have been thoughtfully completed. Brainstorming internal or school issues can be accomplished more expeditiously and with better results after the team has stretched its collective mind outside its immediate boundaries and gained some skill in the technique. Brainstorming internal issues is more sensitive, and even more threatening, for some because it represents areas in which they have control. The team leaders therefore need to lay the groundwork carefully for this part of the brainstorming so that it does not turn into a critique of people or of the way the school is run.

As in the brainstorming of external issues, topics may be stated positively, neutrally, or negatively, referring to strengths or weaknesses, as participants wish. The objective, once again, is to create a list of issues and to see what team members are thinking and what their interests and concerns are. It is often eye-opening for trustees to hear what faculty members are thinking, and vice versa. Diversity within the team contributes to the quality of the list. Although people are not asked to join the team to represent their constituencies as such, they should be encouraged to contribute ideas that they may have heard expressed by colleagues who are not on the planning team.

The same spirit of open-mindedness and goodwill that characterized the previous brainstorming session should prevail here as well. The team leaders need to emphasize the rules for brainstorming, reminding members that, while evaluation and discussion are prohibited, anyone who disagrees with something that is listed may propose the opposite or restate the item in a different way. The lists do not represent any sort of consensus, nor is there any investment in them at this stage. Reminding the team that it will ultimately be developing goals for policy can help in deciding what are legitimate school issues.

School issues generally fall within the following broad categories.

Program
Faculty
Students
Parents
Administration
Plant
Finance
Marketing and public relations
Governance and board of trustees
Other issues specific to the school

Once it has finished listing school issues, the team should be directed to respond to them. The simplest way to organize responses is to use the above list of general categories, adding any that the team wishes. Thus, items having to do with any aspect of the program, curricular or extracurricular, fall into the first category; faculty salaries and benefits, professional development, and teaching loads fall into the second; and so on throughout the list. In this way, all major themes can be brainstormed without having to respond laboriously to each specific item on the lists.

The purpose of the responses to school issues is to challenge the team and to stimulate thinking about change. What are new ways to approach a problem, without having people say "We tried that ten years ago and it didn't work," or "We can't possibly afford that," or "That's not the way we do things here"? The team is given license to create and to dream. Again, responses should begin with verbs and be specific about actions that might be taken in areas of strengths, weaknesses, threats, or opportunities. Even two or three newsprint pages for each general subject will inspire creative thinking.

Even though the team may seem to have opened more doors than it can possibly close, it needs to give time and attention to thorough brainstorming sessions. The entire process is one of winnowing and setting priorities. To try at this point to rank topics or issues is not productive; ranking occurs naturally as the process continues. Avoiding defensiveness and turf guarding at this stage supports the team's ability to look at all elements of the school and to plan more effectively for it.

The school in the future

Considering the school in the future signals the end of the stage in which critical thought, evaluation, and discussion are suspended and marks the beginning of the filtering that will result in formulation of policy goals. It helps for the team to review work accomplished to date, to review the process, and to see what

24

remains to be accomplished. During this stage of the process, team members refine their own visions of the school in the future and share and combine one another's scenarios.

A practical way to make sure that the team plans *for the future* and does not merely solve problems or criticize current practice is to challenge each member to write a vision of the school as it will be in fifteen or twenty years. Schools are, after all, educating young people who will live mostly in the next century. Team members are not being asked to forecast the future but to describe what they would like to see the school be without the constraints that currently exist. Some may object that you can't plan twenty years ahead—which is true—but writing individual scenarios for the school in the future is a means of arriving at a shared vision of the school. The actual implementation plan that develops may be set in increments of one, three, five, or more years. The point is to agree upon long-term mission and goals, then work back to decide what must be done immediately, in the next few years, then five and ten years hence, to reach these goals. This kind of focus is fundamental to the planning process.

Team members should be asked to write their own visions of the school in the future. These visions or scenarios can be built from ideas expressed in the brainstorming sessions as well as from each person's own ideas. A scenario in this sense is a snapshot of the school at a future time; it is visionary in nature and does not revolve around strategies used to achieve desired ends. For instance, if an important item for success in one person's dream is a sizable endowment that makes many things possible, that person need not give details of how the endowment is to be amassed. A scenario may touch on all the elements that comprise the school or just a few that are of particular interest. The composition of the team ensures that little will be overlooked.

Scenarios should be relatively concise, written in no specific format, and cover only several sheets of paper at the most. They are shared with a small group within the team. This marks the beginning of the winnowing and consolidation that will combine the twelve to twenty or so individual scenarios into three or four group scenarios, which will then coalesce into one. (Examples of individual scenarios are given in Appendix E.)

Before moving to the next step, the team leaders divide the team into small groups, whose purpose is to combine individual scenarios. Each group should contain an equal number of team members, mixing trustees, faculty members, parents, and administrators. A team of twelve breaks neatly into three groups, or one of twenty into four, providing for diversity of scenarios but not so many as to be unmanageable. Both team leaders should be part of groups. Each group should contain a balance of perspectives and personalities to produce lively discussion. Each focuses on the topics brought to it by its members.

The tasks for the small groups are to hear the scenarios of all group members and to compare them for areas of agreement and disagreement. The charge to the group is to reach *general* consensus on the main points contained in people's scenarios. Often disagreements arise over specific actions or measures; it helps the group to realize that it should be concentrating on concepts, not details—"What long-term goals do these specific issues support?" That is the group's responsibility at this point, not to decide how those goals might be achieved. For example, rather than specifying test or IQ scores required of candidates for admission, the group should be working on a description of the ideal student.

The aim of the discussions that revolve around the concepts in people's individual scenarios is to reach consensus. If for any reason it becomes obvious that consensus on a given issue will be impossible to reach no matter how long a group talks, the group should mark the issue and move on to others rather than spending all of its time trying to force the impossible. The issue, or issues, on which there was no consensus should be part of the group's report to the whole team. Then, depending on what other groups report, a suitable compromise may become apparent. This topic is enlarged below.

Small-group scenarios, like individual scenarios, are broad-brush, oriented toward the future and general future directions. They should not cite details of school life, for example, or curriculum, administration, or particular people. The directions outlined in the group scenarios should take the form of desired results, not quantifiable measures; those are developed later. They may well be expressed as carrying on things the school already does well, in addition to innovations.

After reaching consensus, each small group decides on and lists the basic elements that it has discussed; this listing becomes the combined group scenario. These basic elements highlight areas of consensus and include major topics on which consensus was not reached. There is no particular format for writing group scenarios, but one simple approach is to outline the group's work on several pages of newsprint from which it will present its report to the team or, if time allows, to type and distribute an outline.

When the small groups complete their work, each designates one person to make its report to the entire planning team. The team's job is to hear all group scenarios; to ask for clarification after each presentation; and, when all have been heard, to compare, contrast, and discuss them in much the same way the small groups did. All the newsprint sheets containing the group scenarios are now posted on the walls of the meeting room. Discussion should focus first on areas of agreement among the scenarios, then on areas of disagreement, trying, if possible, to reach consensus.

Dissenting individuals may now find support for their ideas

in the larger team that they did not find in their small groups. If they do not, the reason may finally be clear. On the other hand, really innovative ideas often require time to incubate. There are ways to make sure that bright ideas rejected by the team but whose time may yet come are not lost. One is to cull them from the brainstorming lists and scenarios and combine them under a heading such as "Ideas not included but worth looking at again" and perhaps even appending the list to the team's report.

Members should be urged to reach consensus on the major items proposed in the group scenarios. It helps to remind the team that it is moving toward the delineation of policy statements for long-range goals. If discussion centers too much on what should actually be implementation strategies, not long-term goals, the team should be encouraged to pay attention to what is eventually to be achieved by those strategies. For example, if members disagree over ways to keep tuition within ranges that will allow the kinds of students the school has always had to continue to afford it, the goal might be stated as developing ways to augment tuition income. The specific means of achieving the goal may be included as suggestions to be explored later when developing actual implementation plans.

Members may be in general agreement on all but one issue, which may have substantial ramifications. In that case, the team might end up recommending to the board a period of time in which to gather supporting data on which to base an informed decision. The planning team at one school, for example, was deadlocked over whether to merge with another school. Realizing that the best service it could perform was to present arguments both for and against the merger, the team finally agreed to recommend that the board embark on a formal study, with a decision to be made within a specified period of time.

One purpose of planning is to raise questions. Some of these cannot be answered by the team or within the span of time the team functions. Questions or issues of this nature should be part of the ensuing report so that they may be answered in a systematic way by those who have the necessary expertise, the authority to make decisions, or both.

Policy goals

When the team has discussed all major topics to its satisfaction, it is time to examine the scenarios for common themes and to translate each theme into a policy goal or goals. The planning process reinforces the distinct but supporting roles of the board and the administration: the board's role is to set school policy; the administration's role is to operate the school within that policy. Therefore, the planning team's recommendations for board approval are appropriately goals for policy; the board's principal role in planning is to be responsible for grand strategy within which actions can be initiated by individuals, committees, and task forces throughout the school.

A policy goal is defined as a positive, comprehensive statement of future direction for a school. Planning teams usually develop one or more policy goals related to program, faculty, students, parents, administration, plant, finance, marketing and public relations, governance, and others unique to the school.

Here is an example of a policy goal related to faculty issues: "To attract, support, and retain outstanding faculty members and to ensure that compensation and working conditions rank at the top of a selective group of comparable schools." One related to plant: "To develop a comprehensive plan to adapt present facilities and add new ones to meet the goals of the academic and nonacademic programs." (Other examples are given in Appendix F.)

As is true in each part of the process, there are several ways to identify and develop policy goals, rationale statements, and suggested implementation plans found in the scenarios for which there is team support. One way is for the team leaders, working at their discretion with the head of the school, to take on the job after the meeting in which group scenarios have been presented and discussed. They then offer their work for review and editing by the team at its next meeting. Another method, almost a necessity in the fast-track retreat approach, is to divide the team into new groups of two or three people and assign each one a topic. Each group is then asked to draft one or more policy goal statements per topic, with elements of a rationale and suggestions for implementation for each policy goal, that all reflect team consensus. Each group can then write goals on newsprint and present them to the team for reactions. By either course, or others that team leaders may devise, a skeleton of a first draft is in place.

The mission statement

The school's mission statement is, quite simply, a succinct description of why the school exists. It is an articulation of the school's purposes and objectives. It expresses the identity that distinguishes the school from other schools. Defining one's mission in the corporate world is as simple and as difficult as answering the question "What is our business?" A good mission statement can imbue a school community with a vision of something strongly desired; it is the heart of planning for the future in an integrated fashion. A clear mission statement delineates not only what a school strives to do but also implies what it should not do. It is the mission statement against which a school seeking accreditation or reaccreditation is evaluated.

Although the mission statement is at the top of the planning hierarchy, the planning process does not begin by examining it. Instead, the process directs attention toward its appraisal after brainstorming, building scenarios, and developing policy goals. If team members began by scrutinizing the school's mission, they might not question some of the basic tenets that should be examined and re-examined periodically.

It may very well be that a planning team will endorse a mission statement that has been in place for years or decades. But it may be that some careful surgery is indicated, or even a complete overhaul. After the team has made its suggestions, the mission statement can be rewritten and brought back to the team. In some schools, protocol may require that the statement go to the faculty or to a faculty committee before it is finally accepted.

The policy goals that are recommended should be consistent with and support the mission statement. It is difficult to evaluate at any given moment whether a school is living up to its mission statement because such a statement tends to be comprehensive and philosophic. But policy goals, though far-reaching, are more specific and, therefore, more easily measured. The implementation plans that are developed to support the policy goals are more specific still and even more easily quantified.

The diagram in Appendix B represents the result of the strategic planning process as a triangle whose apex is the school's mission, supported by the policy goals, established on a base of implementation plans.

The report

Primary responsibility for writing the first draft of the report on the planning process belongs to the head of the school, working with the team leaders. The task is to rewrite and organize the team's work into a coherent draft for its review and editing.

The report should include an annotated list of planning team members, a brief description of the process used, any assumptions on which the report is based, the mission statement, policy goals, the rationale for each, suggestions for implementing each policy goal, and any conclusions.

The list of planning team members should give the names of those making up the team and their relation to the school—faculty member, administrator, trustee, parent, graduate, community resident. Some may have more than one connection; the point is to show the variety of perspectives involved. A very brief description of the process will help readers who were not part of the team, and who may expect something quite different, to understand the team's approach and the result. Because the report itself may be based on certain assumptions not expressed in the body of the report, these should be stated at the outset. The school's mission statement should also be reproduced in the introduction or preface to the report.

Each policy goal should be expressed in a clear, concise statement of a future direction for the school under which strategies that will each help achieve the goal over a period of time can be clustered. Adding the rationale for each goal explains why it is critical to the school's future well-being.

Only *suggestions* for implementation strategies should be included in the report, to show the board what the probable implications of a policy goal might be. Developing actual implementation plans should begin in most cases only after the board has accepted the policy recommendations of the planning team. The report will be most effective if it centers the board's attention on concepts proposed rather than inviting premature scrutiny of actions, some of which it will not even be the board's role to approve. For example, the board would better be asked to consider the implications of developing sources of income other than tuition, at this point, than it would to discuss the merits of particular programs that might be developed. One of the board's concerns about strategic planning might be how concepts are to be translated into actions. To include suggestions for action allows the board to see what strategies might be developed. As various entities in the school are asked to develop their own plans to support policy goals, still other possible strategies will emerge. In all instances, actions that normally require board approval will be brought back to the board when they have been developed in the implementation phase to a point where the board can make an informed decision.

If clear priorities among policy goals did not emerge during the team's discussions, these may be more obvious as the report is being written. If all policy goals are deemed to carry equal weight, then they may simply follow a logical flow. If the first one to appear in the report is the highest priority, that should be made clear either in the report or in the presentation.

Neither length nor weight makes a planning report impressive. The model report is succinct, logical, and compelling in a readable, consistent format. Many schools find that they can address all key points in a dozen pages or less. Volume and complexity detract from a report that is intended to focus on and foster discussion of future directives. If the planning team decides that any kind of additional supporting information is necessary—background information the team was given, financial analyses, segments of the team's work—this should appear in appendixes separate from the body of the report and its recommendations.

When the first draft of the report is complete, copies should be given to team members with a request that general comments and detailed changes be submitted before the next meeting, whose agenda should be to edit the report and to decide the details of how it is to be presented to the board. Since it is entirely possible for a group of intelligent people to argue heatedly over language for an indefinite period of time, limits for discussion are advisable, as is majority rule on changes.

The presentation of the report to the board should be something of an event. Following the cue of the planning team leaders, the head of the school, and the chairman of the board, discussion should center on how the report may best be given to the board. Whether it is to be mailed in advance or will require a special board meeting are questions that might best be answered by looking at the report itself. If certain items might come as a shock to some people, or some really significant changes are recommended, it may be best for board members all to receive the same information at the same time. Because some board members have been part of the planning team, and the team leaders have been reporting to the board throughout the process, the report should not come as a total surprise. The point is to think carefully how best to achieve objective consideration of the draft and subsequent approval. The board may wish to make some additions to or changes in the draft; this adds to their sense of ownership and should be expected. The original composition of the planning team makes it unlikely that such changes will be substantially opposed to the work of the team.

Some thoughts to bear in mind when considering how to present the report to the board are, first, to invite the entire planning team to the meeting where the board will receive the report. Their presence makes visible the team's ecumenical nature and underscores the fact that the recommendations are not those simply of the head, simply of the board chairman, simply of the faculty. Should the board wish to make changes, everyone on the team will better understand the motives for these changes if they have been present for the discussion.

Second, the actual presentation is more effective when various members of the team lead the board through different sections. Some schools use slide shows and have their reports bound; others are more modest. Each school must gauge for itself what will work best.

Third, it is advisable to encourage discussion with team members who are alerted to serve as resource people, perhaps in small-group discussions. Nothing is more deflating than having the board receive the report in silence, thank the team for its work, and then move on to its next agenda item. Formal approval may be scheduled for a subsequent meeting to allow the board to digest the recommendations thoroughly and to have more time for clarification and discussion.

The work of the planning team is complete when it presents its report to the board of trustees.

The primary responsibility of the board in strategic planning is to approve overall policy and to delegate operations to the professionals within the school. The planning team should be precise in asking the board to approve policy goals, not details of suggested implementation plans. With a framework of policy goals in place, the work of designing specific implementation plans can begin. This involves people throughout the school community, as appropriate to a given goal, be they trustees, administrators, faculty members, students, parents, or graduates. Those responsible for carrying out the implementation plans must have a hand in their design—consistent, of course, with the policy goals approved by the board.

Because appraisal and continuous planning are critical to long-term success, the board should carefully consider the planning team's suggestions to determine the most advantageous way of ensuring continuous planning. The planning team's report is designed to be a living document, a management tool for making decisions for the long, medium, and short term.

4
Strategic Action

The strategic action phase of the long-range planning process is composed of the following steps.

> Designing the implementation plan
> Integrating the implementation plan with school finances
> Executing the implementation plan
> Appraising the implementation plan
> Continuous planning

Peter Drucker once remarked that even the best of intentions eventually degenerate into hard work. A strategic plan, no matter how brilliant, is useless if it lacks a sound sequential plan for its execution. The plan must provide for flexibility and adaptability to external events and be perceived internally as valuable: worth the price of committing time, effort, and money.

The implementation plan

Most management literature agrees that the ultimate responsibility for bringing about change in an organization rests with the chief executive officer, whose role has many parallels with that of the head of an independent school. The head should be the principal architect of implementation plans. The head, more than any other person within the school community, has the overall view of how the institution operates and how to use its resources well.

In developing an implementation plan, the head needs to work with others: the board chairman, other board officers and committees, members of the administration, faculty members and committees, parents' and graduates' associations, and student leaders.

Each policy goal needs to be supported by a set of objectives, tactics, or strategies that delineate who does what, when, and how, include quantifiable measures, assign resources, give beginning and end dates, and specify where final authority lies. Plans should be sequential, indicating what can realistically be done this year, next year, in five years, and beyond. In this way, further priorities are set. (Examples of implementation plans and a format for organizing them are given in Appendix G.)

First steps after a major planning effort often consist of directives to study, review, and do research. In some cases, outside professional help is needed to develop certain details, such as master planning for the physical plant, an ambitious endowment, a capital campaign, new approaches to curriculum development. The results of this background analysis then go to the appropriate level—board, head, curriculum committee—for an informed decision.

Each strategy or action should be assigned to individuals by name or title or to committees or task forces. Each action should be allotted a reasonable amount of time to get under way and be completed. Some will culminate in a report that leads to further action. As with personnel, resources should be assigned as needed.

Long-range planning need not involve rampant proliferation of committees. A school's existing structure should be used as much as possible; ad hoc or permanent committees should be created only when no others can assume additional duties.

Not everything in the plan requires board approval; many actions fall within the head's authority or the faculty's purview. Other actions, particularly for goals related to the composition of the board and the way it functions, or for major fund raising, for example, are purely in the board's province. The board should design implementation plans for policy goals that relate directly to it and police its own progress on strategic action.

Integrating plan and finances

A budget is a detailed guide for action that sets financial standards and provides a quantitative basis for monitoring performance within a specific length of time, usually one year. Conversely, the strategic plan is a much longer, far less detailed, conceptual plan that identifies the mission and long-term goals of the school. The annual budget should be consistent with the plan and provide for addressing segments of the long-term recommendations as well as provide the wherewithal for implementing those recommendations.

It is critical to determine the extent of the relation of the budget to the strategic plan and to integrate only those items that are suitable. Budget demands can cripple the plan. Key points to remember are that the budgeting process should support overall strategy—not the reverse—and that the strategic plan is by definition a long-range plan that goes beyond the range of annual budgeting and several-year financial forecasting.

Computer-generated spreadsheet analyses can help the school manipulate options and help in determining how long the school might realistically need to meet goals and objectives related to faculty compensation, capital expenditures, tuition levels, and other significant areas of the budget.

Although long-range planning does not always result in capital campaigns, building programs, and extensive fund raising, most recommendations will in some manner affect the school's financial picture and test the board's commitment to fund raising.

Executing the plan

Whether the planning team recommends significant change in the school or not, change will take place without any kind of planning. And often a school must change its present strategies just to continue what it has done successfully in the past. Research shows that organizations resist even change that is perceived as beneficial and highly desirable. For this reason, people who are to be involved in carrying out plans must be involved at some point in designing them. A sense of ownership by faculty members and administrators helps to minimize resistance. Keeping key people in the school community informed during the strategic planning and strategic action phases of the planning process is beneficial. For example, if there are persons who are perceived to have influence and a measure of control, even if in community good will alone, and who are no longer formally connected with the school or with the planning process, a courtesy visit to them by the head and board chairman before the plan is made final or at pivotal stages later on can reap immeasurable benefits.

Much of the current management literature inundating bookstores would have us believe that implementation planning is all. Obviously no one wants a plan that accumulates dust on the shelf, but a good strategic plan *must* precede action. Perhaps one reason so many plans are shelved is that the conceptual strategic plan was so poorly developed that implementation was virtually impossible. Sound strategic planning gives direction and definition to the resulting plan for action.

Action consists, obviously, of carrying out the plans designed in the preceding step. Almost everyone in the school may be involved in some way, although strategic planning is not concerned with every single component that makes a school run smoothly. Just as activity in a school does not cease until a well-formulated plan is in place, no matter how important the plan might be, much will be business as usual. As chief architect of the implementation plan, the head of the school is also its primary coordinator.

Appraising the plan

A critical function of effective planning is to frame a practical system of review and appraisal. An implementation plan is an internal management document that is by its nature subject to change. It reflects the separate but supporting responsibility of the board for policy and of the head for operations within the guidelines of established policy. If good workmanship has created a clear, cogent plan, one would hope for clocklike precision in its execution.

Simply having a first-rate plan does not guarantee success, however; strategies designed to minimize threats or to take advantage of opportunities may be quite successful one year but not the next. A faculty committee devising sweeping curricular changes or a parents' association task force creating a program to improve communications with members may have worked with diligence but not have met its deadlines. Yet another group addressing faculty benefits may have come up with a new approach for which money was not available. Objective appraisal and analysis helps to determine what is not working and identify possible solutions.

Appraisal of progress toward goals is as important for those tactics that work as it is for those that do not. Specific plans should include the elements on which they can be evaluated: Did the strategy, tactic, or objective produce the desired result? Was it begun and completed on schedule? Was enough time allowed? Were enough people assigned? Was enough money budgeted? If the task is still going on, is it on schedule? And if to any of these questions the answer is no, why not? What can be changed to achieve the desired results?

This kind of inquiry, whether done once or twice a year, can help maintain the momentum of the original plan. Responsibility for oversight can be assigned to a board standing committee or to an ad hoc committee formed especially for this purpose, or the original planning team may be reconvened to perform the task, depending on which is most suitable to the school and its structure. The role of the oversight group is to review implementation plans systematically to see what is working and what is not, to prescribe as needed, and to make suggestions to the head for periodic updating of the plan and reporting to the board. A dispassionate, uncritical attitude on the part of the group will help appraisal to function smoothly.

The first year or two after a substantial planning effort, most of the work of appraisal centers around implementation plans. It is satisfying to check off what has been achieved, to bestow compliments, and to proceed to new or subsequent plans for achieving overall goals or, in time, for proposing new goals to replace those that have become outdated.

Continuous planning

As time passes, those involved in appraisal must remain aware of external events and alert to signals of significant internal or external changes that have implications for the strategic plan even though it has a certain amount of flexibility built into it.

As substantial change in external or internal events affects any of the assumptions of the strategic plan, it may be well to begin the process again, revamping it to build on the foundations of the obsolete plan. Examples of changes that could make repetition of the entire process seem advisable are serious economic reverses in the community, a change in school leadership, the fact that many of those who participated in and "owned" the plan have moved on. Or, as another example, if the major portion of the school's energy has been dedicated to fund raising or a major building project and a sense of renewal is evident, the time might be right for recapturing some of the original enthusiasm and momentum by reactivating the process to see what has been accomplished and to decide where the school might next direct its energies and resources.

Appraising goals and objectives need not be laborious or time-consuming. The head has most of the information at hand and can simply annotate copies of the plan to expedite a meeting of the oversight group. A more lengthy appraisal might take place at a board retreat, where the head and others would report on progress and the rest of the time could be devoted to brainstorming changes that have taken place since the plan was written or last appraised, with suggestions for how to keep it rolling.

It is critical to keep planning alive. Appraisal and continuous planning should become part of the management of the institution. Regular updating of information is a key factor in effective appraisal, as is objective assessment of strategies. Planning continuously can help the school anticipate events rather than simply react to them.

A new head of school does not necessarily mean than an existing plan should be scrapped. However, opportunities should be created for the new head to respond to the plan from a fresh perspective and to make an imprint on the plan.

5
Parting Words

A process is only a process; it is the people who adapt it to their particular circumstances who make it work. Strategic planning offers opportunities at all stages for the school to tailor the process to the school's own needs.

If, for instance, broader involvement in the brainstorming phase is seen as advantageous, planning team leaders can arrange sessions with the faculty, the student body, and the governing boards of the parents' and graduates' associations to get reactions to the team's work and supplement its efforts. Similarly, asking student groups to create scenarios for the school's future can produce interesting and unexpected results. A good rule of thumb, however, is not to solicit what is not really wanted or will not be used. Planning team leaders should be sincere in asking for information from others. As a corollary, the team has an obligation to keep those informed whom it has asked for their counsel.

The planning team may find that at some point during the process it cannot move forward or resolve an issue without more specific information. The team should seek out sources and report back as soon as possible, always bearing in mind the distinction between background information and hard data that should properly be gathered later as part of the implementation phase.

The examples of timetables and agendas given in Appendix C are also subject to variation, depending on the particular needs of the school. Each school must decide what will work best in already overloaded schedules. There is no one right way to proceed, and it is true that "no time is a good time" for planning. Once the decision is made to commit the time and effort to planning, shortchanging will create frustration and inferior results. Time spent in organizing the planning is time very well spent.

Techniques for leading the team through identifying policy goals and supporting information vary with personalities and skills. Regardless how policy goals are drawn from the work that leads to them, wise team leaders will make sure that there is genuine team consensus and support for the directions expressed by the goals before proceeding.

It is up to the leaders to keep the various constituencies of the school community informed about the work of the planning team. Although some confidentiality is involved, key people at least should be told what is developing as the process evolves. People are apt to reject out of hand things that come as a complete surprise, particularly if they suggest the potential for change.

Other decisions need to be made: number of planning team participants, locations for working sessions, frequency of meetings, the format of the report, methods of presenting the report to the board, the shape and specificity of implementation plans, and ways of involving people who are responsible for executing plans in their design. Each team will make its choices by thinking about what will be best for the school. The process has integrity; to treat one area out of context destroys that integrity. Similarly, the planning process is not a recipe that always produces uniform results.

A word of caution

Strategic planning is not a panacea. There are limitations in the process itself, in the manner in which it may be applied, and in the results.

A major pitfall is disillusionment, which can be caused by failure to match individual expectations of what the process can do or by the overwhelming nature of the difference between what a school would like to do and what seems realistic now. At the risk of sounding either fatuous or evangelistic, the concept of self-fulfilling prophecies often does work. In *Seven Tomorrows,* based on information compiled for the futures group at SRI International, John Hawken, James Ogilvy, and Peter Schwartz tell how negative futures can be changed by actions that are spurred by the negative face of forecast future options.

A good example is what happened in this country when shortages of various energy and fuel sources were predicted; people did work with and change, at least for the time being, what were dire scenarios. This is not to deny that some situations seem to be without much hope, or that some circumstances deteriorate so far that not much can be done to reverse them. In some instances, however, defining the breadth and depth of the obstacle to be overcome and laying out an orderly plan of attack is all that planning can achieve.

Another pitfall is trying to substitute long-range planning when crisis management is what is really needed. The best time to engage in strategic planning is when no crises are impending; otherwise, the exercise will be centered around the crises, and effective planning will be impossible.

Yet another trap is to use long-range planning to carry out a hidden agenda. If the real but unstated aim is to point out weaknesses in the head or in other people, for example, it is best to address the problem straightforwardly before initiating the planning process.

Another inhibitor to productive planning work is in the nature of the relations that develop within the planning team. Ideally, team members are creative people who are committed to and knowledgeable about the school and are respected by their colleagues. Although they may meet all these criteria, some people simply cannot work within a disciplined process whose purpose is to raise questions that involve ambiguity, cannot think in broad enough terms, or think that such complexities make consensus impossible. The involvement of such people, whether board members, faculty members, or others, often becomes counterproductive. Their opinions and contributions can be sought in other ways.

The planning process seeks to keep options open as long as necessary and not to foreclose on specific issues that need further consideration. Even so, there is not time to dwell on every topic to the satisfaction of all concerned; topics that resist consensus may be assigned to individuals, committees, or task forces so that conclusions may be hammered out and integrated into the plan. The purpose of planning is to raise questions that may cause dissent. The participants must be able, to the best of their ability, to channel dissension productively.

The degree of confidentiality within the process varies from school to school. At the very least, team members should refrain from announcing conclusions until the report is written, edited by the planning team, and approved by the board. Discussion of points taken out of context could impair the credibility of the report in the minds of people not fully acquainted with it. This is not to say that the team should conduct its proceedings under a veil of secrecy, which is impossible in most schools, anyway. It should, however, be careful about making casual comments that could raise false expectations, give innovative strategies to competitors, or preclude objective, thoughtful evaluation of the final report. One example would be a team member who states that faculty salaries are going to be raised substantially—a statement for which there will be enthusiasm in some quarters—without adding that the plan for raising salaries is to be carried out over a designated period of time, not all at once. Another example would be for a team member to remark that the school is interested in acquiring a particular piece of property, thereby alerting others who are interested and perhaps thus affecting the sale price. One of the most efficient parts of any school is the rumor mill. The planning team should be cautioned not to feed it.

Failure to orient the planning team sufficiently toward the future has negative results, not because personalities or current operations may be seen as ineffective, but because the focus is too narrow and shortsighted.

An inability to clarify and distinguish between the roles of the board and head results in confusion at every level. Similarly, failure to delineate where a school wants to go before deciding how to get there causes frustration and disorder. Further, failure to translate policy goal statements into measurable action or to involve those responsible for carrying out plans in designing them can bring about a breakdown in communications and resistance to or interruption of logical action.

These are only some of the pitfalls encountered by schools in the planning process. In the final analysis, the sensitivity, perceptiveness, and skill of the leaders of the planning team will steer an adroit course around the obstacles that haunt the hours of strategic planning. People, not the process, make planning successful.

Benefits
The benefits gained from engaging in strategic planning and policy development are many. Not the least is the strategic plan

itself and the supporting operating plan, which charts short-, medium-, and long-range implementation steps. At its simplest, planning for the future ensures that there *will be* a future.

In addition to benefits discussed earlier, several additional ones need emphasis. Among them are the good will and positive working relations that grow within a planning team. Outside of parent-teacher conferences, school meetings, routine business, or the usual yearly social gatherings, board members, faculty members, and administrators have few opportunities to meet together, let alone collaborate. Everyone involved learns more about the school, and the community gains new insights and perspectives on its operations.

The strategic plan—but not the implementation plan—may be shared throughout the school community and the wider community as well. It is a good focus for a parents' or graduates' association meeting, perhaps followed by an invitation for general discussion. Many schools distribute brochures based on the strategic plan as part of their marketing and public relations effort.

A good strategic plan is essential for fund raising. It has been suggested by some that fund-raising needs alone are sufficient reason to engage in planning. Projecting a clear picture of a shared vision for a school is a powerful fund-raising tool. It demonstrates to the potential giver that the school has thought carefully about its future and that the donor can help make that dream a reality. Successful capital campaigns rest squarely on the foundation of a well-prepared strategic plan as evidence that funds to be raised will help in carrying out a logical, consistent master plan and that the school did its homework before soliciting money.

The greatest value derived from strategic planning comes from the school's planning for itself. Although outside help may be sought from time to time, nothing substitutes for a school's planning for itself.

Appendix A.
Bibliography

Cited in the text

Drucker, Peter F. *The Age of Discontinuity: Guidelines to Our Changing Society.* New York: Harper & Row, 1969.

Drucker, Peter F. *Managing in Turbulent Times.* New York: Harper & Row, 1980.

Hawken, Paul, James Ogilvy, and Peter Schwartz. *Seven Tomorrows: Toward a Voluntary History.* New York: Bantam Books, 1982.

Hawley, Richard A. *The Headmaster's Papers.* Middlebury, Vt.: Paul S. Eriksson, 1983.

Trustee Handbook, 5th ed. Boston: National Association of Independent Schools, 1983.

Selected additional readings

America in Perspective: Major Trends in the United States through the 1990's. Oxford Analytica. Boston: Houghton Mifflin, 1986.

American Demographics. Published monthly. Subscription information: P.O. Box 6543, Syracuse NY 13217.

Diebold, John. *Making the Future Work: Unleashing Our Powers of Innovation for the Decades Ahead.* New York: Simon & Schuster, 1984.

Drucker, Peter F. *Innovation and Entrepreneurship: Practice and Principles.* New York: Harper & Row, 1985.

Garreau, Joel. *Nine Nations of North America.* New York: Avon, 1981.

Hawken, Paul. *The Next Economy.* New York: Holt, Rinehart and Winston, 1983.

Appendix A

Hodgkinson, Harold L. *All One System: Demographics of Education, Kindergarten through Graduate School.* 1985. Institute for Educational Leadership, Inc., 1001 Connecticut Ave. NW, Suite 310, Washington DC 20036.

Mitchell, Arnold. *The Nine American Lifestyles: Who We Are and Where We Are Going.* New York: Macmillan, 1983.

Peters, Thomas J., and Robert H. Waterman, Jr. *In Search of Excellence: Lessons from America's Best-Run Companies.* New York: Harper & Row, 1982.

Sizer, Theodore R. *Horace's Compromise: The Dilemma of the American High School.* Boston: Houghton Mifflin, 1984.

World Future Society. *The Futurist.* Published bimonthly. Subscription information: 4916 St. Elmo Ave., Bethesda MD 20814.

World Future Society. *Through the 80's: Thinking Globally, Acting Locally.* Ed. Frank Feather. Bethesda, Md., 1980.

World Future Society Bulletin. Published bimonthly. Subscription information: 4916 St. Elmo Ave., Bethesda MD 20814.

Appendix B.
Process Outline and Diagram

Outlined, the four-phase strategic planning and policy development process appears as follows.

I. **Preparing for planning**
   A. Planning team
   B. Timetable
   C. Logistics

II. **Strategic planning**
   A. Considering the external climate
   B. Considering the internal climate
   C. Defining the school in the future
   D. Identifying policy goals
   E. Appraising the school's mission statement
   F. Preparing and presenting a report

III. **Strategic action**
   A. Designing the implementation plan
   B. Integrating the implementation plan with school finances
   C. Executing the implementation plan
   D. Appraising the implementation plan

IV. **Continuous planning**

A diagram of the strategic planning process appears as follows.

Appendix B

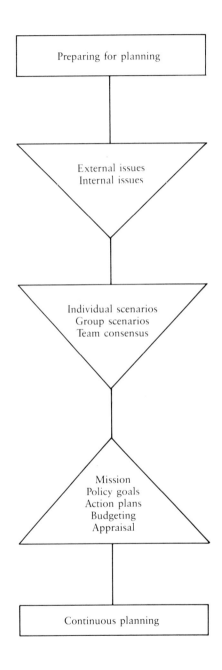

Preparing for planning

External issues
Internal issues

Individual scenarios
Group scenarios
Team consensus

Mission
Policy goals
Action plans
Budgeting
Appraisal

Continuous planning

Appendix C.
Sample Timetables

The portion of the strategic planning and policy development process required to generate a report for the board can range from several days to most of a school year. In the case of boarding schools, where trustees who should participate in the process usually do not live conveniently close to the school, it is impractical to talk of seven or eight sessions spanning a period of several months. Day schools have more flexibility, because their trustees usually live within easy commuting distance. Schools can easily adapt any of these schedules to their needs, allowing more or less time during or between meetings and adding meetings if necessary.

Here are detailed timetables for the three basic approaches to planning described in Chapter 2: fast track, flexible timetable, and school year.

Fast track

Step	Deadline	Responsibility
Getting started	August	Head, board chairman, team leaders
Retreat	Late September	Team leaders, team
Draft of report	October	Head or drafting team
Further editing	November	Head, team leaders, team
Report to board	December	Team leaders, team
Design implementation plan	January	Head and others designated
Appraisal	Semiannual	Head, executive committee (or designated group)

To use the fast-track approach successfully, the retreat must be very well organized and have a timed agenda. The minimum working time needed, exclusive of breaks, is sixteen hours. The retreat leader(s) must be highly skilled, and, because participants must understand the time constraints, it helps to emphasize that the purpose of the retreat is *only* to create overall strategy. Many schools have used the fast-track approach. Their reports do not seem to differ in quality from those produced according to other timetables. Following is a more detailed schedule for the fast track.

Day 1 (retreat)
Orientation
Consider external climate
Consider internal climate
Create individual scenarios
Create small-group scenarios

Day 2 (retreat)
Present small-group scenarios to planning team
Discuss and reach consensus on major points
Discuss implementation plans
Discuss contents of report to board

Subsequent meeting (separated from the first two by several weeks)
Approve report from drafts written and circulated in the interim
Plan strategy for presenting report to the board
Rehearse presentation

Present report to board

Flexible timetable

Step	*Deadline*	*Responsibility*
Getting started	January	Head, board chairman, team leaders
Planning team meetings	February and March	Team leaders and team
Draft of report completed	April	Head or drafting team
Report to board	May	Team leaders, team
Design action plans	Summer	Head and others designated
Appraisal	Annually	Head, standing committee

The flexible timetable represents a very reasonable schedule that allows time to get typescripts to team members between meetings as well as time to reflect and gather additional data. This timetable works especially well for day schools. The main disadvantage is that it tends to be difficult to find dates and times that suit all team members' calendars.

Meeting 1 (four to six hours)
Orientation
Brainstorming
  Consider external climate
  Consider internal climate; responses
Give instructions for scenarios

Meeting 2 (approximately two weeks later; two to three hours)
Form groups
Present individual scenarios to groups
Discuss scenarios, reach consensus
Define basic elements in group scenarios

Meeting 3 (approximately two weeks later, with groups meeting in the interim as needed; two to three hours)
Present group scenarios to full team
Discuss similarities and differences
Reach consensus
Make preliminary identification of policy goals
Assign writing of first draft

Meeting 4 (several weeks later; two to three hours)
Critique first draft
Refine and restate policy goals as needed
Discuss implementation plans
Assign writing of second draft, to include suggested implementation plans

Meeting 5 (several weeks later; two hours)
Fine tune and approve second draft
Discuss strategy for presenting report to board

Meeting 6 (next scheduled or specially called board meeting)
Present report to board

Appendix C

The school year, beginning in October

Week 1: Meeting
Orientation
Brainstorm national and local issues

Week 4: Meeting
Brainstorm internal issues

Week 6: Meeting
Review all brainstorming lists
Introduce scenario concept
Form groups

Week 8: Meeting
Discuss policy goal concept
Groups hear individual scenarios
Groups determine own meeting schedule

Weeks 9-11: Groups meet on own

Christmas break

Weeks 11-14: Groups meet on own as needed

Week 15: Retreat (if a retreat is impractical, allow another week or two)
Present group models to full team
Begin synthesizing models
Discuss implementation plans
Select one model for presentation

Week 17: Meeting
Present first draft of report to team
Finish implementation plans

Week 20: Meeting
Approve final draft of report
Design strategy for presenting report to board

Week 22: (or next scheduled board meeting)
Present report to board

Appendix D.
Brainstorming

Brainstorming lists from the planning process of schools vary with the nature of each school, the region of the country in which it is located, community characteristics, and the backgrounds and personalities of planning team members.

The length of brainstorming lists differs primarily according to the amount of time allotted. Following are a few examples in each of the major brainstorming categories taken from the much longer lists compiled by the planning team of a Middle Atlantic boarding school.

International/national issues
 1. National concern over education
 2. Global competitiveness
 3. Foreign debt
 4. Oil prices
 5. Nuclear threat
 6. Women in the work force
 7. Shifting population centers
 8. Changes in family structure
 9. Quality of life
10. Waning church influence
11. Drugs and alcohol
12. Power of the media
13. Growth of the national debt
14. Welfare society
15. Changing job opportunities

16. Technology
17. Longer lives; multiple careers
18. Environmental concerns
19. Change in tax structure
20. Immigration
21. Information economy
22. Latchkey children
23. Stress
24. Terrorism
25. Aging population

Local issues
1. Population growth
2. Land-use plans
3. Mass transit
4. Controlled development
5. Increasing control of independent schools by state and local governmental entities
6. Health
7. Isolated community
8. Conservative nature of community
9. Town/gown
10. Building costs
11. Availability of labor
12. Climate
13. Beauty
14. Resources of and closeness to Washington, D.C.
15. Competition for regional students
16. Relationship of public and private schools
17. Community image
18. Social pressures
19. Availability of good medical services
20. Tourism
21. Available sports facilities
22. Secondary school educator pool
23. Cost of energy
24. Housing
25. Real estate costs

Following are some sample responses to just two of the major themes that surfaced from the brainstorming on local issues.

Responses to local issues

Regulation of independent schools
 1. Lobby against
 2. Accommodate
 3. Ignore
 4. Coordinate nationally
 5. Communicate with school constituency
 6. Join forces with other area schools
 7. Invite people in authority to visit campus
 8. Be sensible and patient
 9. Throw the rascals out; elect new officials
10. Rally community leadership

The environment
 1. Develop land-use plan
 2. Develop conservation curriculum
 3. Clean up roadside litter
 4. Rally local residents to environmental issues
 5. Sponsor a conference on conservation
 6. Monitor county politics on environmental issues and advocate our position
 7. Design a landscape plan around indigenous flora and fauna
 8. Draw on Environmental Protection Agency resources
 9. Don't sell any more land
10. Consider using part of land as a wildlife preserve

School issues
 1. Size
 2. Community service
 3. Recruitment
 4. Faculty salaries
 5. Tradition
 6. Faculty housing
 7. Clarity of purpose
 8. Parent involvement
 9. Gender balance—faculty and staff

10. Balanced budget
11. Tuition
12. Energy plan
13. Curriculum development
14. College counseling
15. Sports
16. Library
17. Efficient use of existing buildings
18. Year-round use of buildings
19. Constructive alternatives for leisure time
20. Financial aid
21. Minority recruitment—faculty and student
22. Roles of board and head
23. Board recruitment and training
24. Fund raising—annual and capital
25. Professional development for faculty

Following are some of the responses to two of the nine categories established as major themes in the school issues list.

Responses to school issues

Program
1. Concentrate on thinking and learning skills
2. Promote interdisciplinary approaches
3. Emphasize student responsibility in all aspects of the program
4. Strengthen community service program
5. Organize visiting scholar program
6. Develop long-term curriculum for changing student body
7. Emphasize diversity in students and faculty
8. Build a fine arts center
9. Increase computer use
10. Involve more graduates in yearly program

Faculty
1. Develop faculty and staff equity program
2. Increase salaries and benefits
3. Devise system for more direct contact with parents
4. Clarify role of faculty council

5. Encourage participation in professional associations; allow time and money
6. Create a faculty enrichment program
7. Identify several other schools with whom our faculty can have regular professional exchanges
8. Consider sabbatical leaves
9. Improve housing
10. Refine the faculty evaluation system

Appendix E.
Individual Scenarios

Following are excerpts from scenarios written by members of a planning team for a coeducational day-boarding school in New England.

Scenario 1

I have had some serious difficulties in deciding what form in which to record my conclusions and, second, in making myself actually do it. I'm not sure why, for I could write volumes. My dreams and expectations for our school are immense, and I believe real opportunities are virtually endless.

It occurs to me that my problem is trying to play God for a ten-year plan, and therefore I fear making a mistake in that divine plan. I take solace, however, in the thought that "my plan" will be filtered, torn apart, changed, and so reconstructed with others as to make it unrecognizable. On the other hand, I have had my small input into the process.

Final note: I am, personally, most goal-oriented, and must work toward short- and long-term goals. "My plan," therefore, is as I see the school fifteen years from now with figures and descriptions rather than a well-constructed scheme presenting my dreams and expectations.

Final, final note: Three dates seem important to me. First, 1991: the 125th anniversary of the founding of the school; second, 1993 (ten years ahead); and third, 1998 (the year the head becomes sixty-five). The last date is to me the most significant one and, therefore, the basis of my making a fifteen-year plan.

And, so, on to the task.

Scenario 2

There are 650 students at the school. This is the minimum number to sustain the massive investment in electronics that is now a major factor in education. Many of the basic subjects are taught through electronic programs developed by educational associations and commercial publishers. The faculty, although large, will fall in ratio to the number of students. Teachers will spend less time on the basics and more on discussion groups, counsel students with independent projects, and take continuing education courses to cope with ever-growing fields of knowledge. Published reference materials will also be transmitted more and more by electronic media.

To cope with this new educational format, two basic facilities will be built. The first is an information center, where the electronic equipment will be housed and basic courses taught. The second is a larger, sophisticated science center, where students will learn the skills needed for a high-tech America. Science will not just be for those with a bent. All students will take courses in mathematics (through calculus), physics, chemistry, biology, and genetics, with every student having a science major.

The humanities will not be ignored. History will be taught with a heavy emphasis on current problems. Historical perspective will be a discarded luxury. Since more of recent history has been documented on film, electronic media will be used extensively.

The school will continue its emphasis on athletics. One or two additional hockey rinks will be built, and the school will become a hockey center for neighboring institutions. Because of heavy scholastic pressures, many students will go out for only one or two sports a year. A special program will be organized for the nonathlete, with an emphasis on strength and endurance so that all students may take pride in their physical abilities.

The school will step up its effort to recruit more middle class and minority students. There will be more scholarships and loans available as a result of our intensive development program. The school, together with other independent schools, will sponsor an independent primary school in the inner city. This will provide a model of what hard work and little money can accomplish.

The school will not become a refuge from a public education system that has failed. It must be in the vanguard of America's education revival. It must serve its students, its faculty, and, most of all, its community.

Appendix E

Scenario 3

In ten or fifteen years I see the school still following its basic goals but with a stronger program to achieve those goals.

The overall program will still be balanced between preparing students for the world of advanced education and developing an attitude of caring and understanding for family, for the community, and for the world.

Over the next ten or twelve years, competition among secondary schools will have increased significantly, as will the total cost of education relative to the cost of living. A combination of escalating costs and competition will have forced ongoing re-examination of and improvements in curriculum and faculty output.

A new creed will have been adopted at the school to remind all concerned that "Of those to whom much is given much is expected." Incoming students and their families will be judged on their willingness to accept this creed. They will be reminded that the kind of education this school offers is not something to which one is entitled but is an investment in the future — the biggest one they will ever be asked to make. This education will require a significant contribution on the part of faculty, students, and parents.

Size and mix. The school in the mid 1990's will have a student body of about 500. It will still be primarily a day school, but will have a boarding program designed to enhance the day program. Many of the boarders will be minority students.

The student body will be evenly divided between boys and girls and will include from 10 to 15 per cent minority students. Family backgrounds will be as diverse as possible but representative of our neighboring constituencies. Thanks to new resources, tuition constraints will not be as severe as they were in the mid 1980's.

A highly skilled admission office will project the image of the school in such a way that it will be able to meet and overcome the competition in securing what we consider to be excellence — an inquisitive mind, interest in the community, generalists.

Program. Thanks to a complete recent evaluation of curriculum, with annual re-evaluations thereafter, the school's program will become more flexible and responsive to changing times.

The "basics" will still be the foundation of curriculum, but more courses will be offered to prepare students for the world of technology and decision-making sciences that will face them. There will be more required courses in the basics, but the definition of the basics will have been expanded to include science and technology.

The computer will be used to permit faculty members to reach more students more effectively. Large lecture courses will be given, with shared faculty members from other schools lecturing on their specialties.

Athletics will be an important part of the program, but with much less emphasis on interschool competition and securing the best athletes.

Some form of community involvement will be mandatory in the junior and senior years, with introductory issue-oriented courses in the freshman and sophomore years.

Courses on chemical dependency and sexuality will be mandatory and, if possible, will include parents when appropriate.

Faculty. In the mid 1990's, the faculty will be about the same size as it was in the early 1980's, but the administrative tasks currently performed by the teaching faculty will be performed by professional administrators and computers. In this way, the ratio of faculty to students will, as a practical matter, have increased and the faculty will be able to spend more time on student teaching and working directly with students.

Faculty compensation will be more competitive with the business world, in part because of new programs designed to help teachers obtain adequate housing and retirement benefits. Loan programs will provide teachers with housing loans, and there will be more on-campus housing, some of which will be rented to faculty members at less than market rates.

As compensation to faculty members increases, the evaluation process will become more refined. Evaluation and continuing education will be a way of life for all teachers, and faculty turnover will increase.

Much will be expected of the faculty in teaching the goals of the school and not just in providing a better than average college preparation.

Financial support. Thanks to a major fund-raising drive at the height of the last bull market and a very successful deferred giving program, the endowment fund stands at about $50 million.

Endowment income, having expanded almost tenfold, has become the source of increases in faculty compensation and a variety of different forms of financial aid.

The support of the neighboring high-tech industry has been very important in bringing in additional funds.

Appendix E

Scenario 4

The greatest single change in program came with the building of the XYZ Computer Science Institute. The only facility of its kind on secondary school education, it continues to keep the application pool at peak levels. It is staffed and equipped to provide the best preparation in computer technology and software at the high school level, and its program rivals that provided in many colleges. During the summer months it is used as a summer school for student computer literacy, a teacher-training facility, and a center for business seminars in computer science. It has generated both interest and income and is a prototype for computer science in education.

The school program underwent changes that resulted in the following.

1. Tightening of the curriculum with more basic requirements: two foreign languages by graduation; more mathematics, science, and history; drama a required course in new communications area of English department; art and music required.

2. All electives re-evaluated, with some given on Friday afternoon or Saturday on a fee basis.

3. A four-day physical fitness (athletic) program, with shorter seasons for each sport; more emphasis on noncompetitive and lifetime sports—sailing, skiing, dance, ice skating; nutrition; emphasis on social interaction.

4. The fifth day: club meetings, cultural trips, community involvement, library, tutoring, adviser meetings, apprenticeships.

5. Manual labor: grounds maintenance as an alternative to athletics.

6. Guidance department for testing, evaluation, counseling in career choices.

Appendix F.
Policy Goals

Following are examples of policy goals developed by schools in five regions of the country.

Elementary school in the Southwest

Students

To enroll and retain a preschool through grade 5 student body of strong academic and personal potential and of diverse backgrounds and experiences.

Program

To provide a strong academic program, within a caring and supportive environment, complemented by enrichment opportunities over the course of a twelve-month school year.

Faculty

To offer fully competitive compensation and benefits in order to attract and retain teachers of top caliber from diverse backgrounds.

To develop more avenues for continued enrichment and educational growth so that teaching at the school remains a fulfilling experience.

Parents

To encourage strong involvement of parents in their children's education.

Development and community relations

To develop and promote contributions made to the community by the school.

To establish relationships that are mutually beneficial to the school and all its publics.

To provide the mechanisms for raising funds to carry forth the goals of the long-range plan.

Plant

While retaining the school's aesthetic qualities, to expand and improve its physical plant to meet the needs of the educational program and to provide an urban oasis for the children.

Finance

To secure financial resources to carry out the policies and programs of the school while adhering to sound fiscal practices.

Administration

To provide leadership for the accomplishment of board policies and the master plan.

To facilitate open communication between the administration and all other segments of the school community.

To provide, retain, and support a small but energetic administration comprising a mixture of personalities led by a forward-looking, strong, and diplomatic head.

To provide instructional leadership.

To supervise and evaluate programs, faculty, and staff.

To develop and adhere to the school's budget.

Board

To select members with the necessary skills who will expend effort and raise funds for the school, and to plan for the board's continuity.

To achieve financial stability through long-range planning.

To review and adopt policies that support the mission statement, the long-range plan, and the master plan.

To employ, retain, and support a forward-looking, strong, and diplomatic head.

To investigate the efficacy of expansion to other areas of the city.

Coeducational K-12 day school in the Southeast

Goal A. The school will attract and retain a student body of 475-500 students of high potential, ability, and diverse background. This size will enable the school to provide a full range of academic programs and to use the existing facility to the fullest possible extent.

Goal B. The school will seek to attract and retain well-qualified faculty members and to provide levels of compensation competitive with local public schools. The school will establish a regular program of faculty development and evaluation.

Goal C. The school will continue to provide rigorous programs in basic, traditional curriculum areas. The school will also provide substantive programs at all levels in fine arts, foreign language, and technological advances.

Goal D. The school will provide a facility suitable to accommodate its enrollment and will provide appropriate space to implement its curriculum and stated goals.

Goal E. Income from tuition and fees will cover the operating costs reflected in the annual budget.

Goal F. The board of trustees will maintain an aggressive total development program encompassing all areas of fund raising in order to provide appropriate facilities and scholarship funds and to meet special program needs.

Goal G. Nonacademic, extracurricular, and special programs will be provided in sufficient number and variety so that all members of the school community may develop personal talents, physical fitness, career interests, and positive social skills through interaction with others.

Goal H. The board of trustees will be representative of the school's constituency and will provide for outside representation.

Boys' elementary and secondary school in the Middle Atlantic

Reaffirmations

The school's role as a college preparatory school should continue to be given high priority.

The school must seek to attract and retain the best possible faculty, which should reflect the diversity of the student body.

The school should seek to provide appropriate opportunities for the infusion of new students in all school divisions. The school should strengthen its search for increased diversity among its students, while maintaining admission standards consistent with its program.

The school must continue its efforts to foster moral and ethical growth

Appendix F

among its students, with emphasis on the basic values of integrity, consideration for others, and the courage of one's convictions.

Recognizing that athletics are an integral and important aspect of the educational program, continue a strong athletic program.

Recognizing that extracurricular activities are an integral part of the educational program, the school should continue and build upon an activities program that stresses teamwork, interdependency, and interpersonal skills, and that emphasizes citizenship and responsibility.

Administer the school in the most economic and efficient fashion possible, consistent with its goals and mission.

New dimensions

The school should foster increased association between boys and girls both on campus and off.

In order to meet most effectively the changing needs of the student body and to encourage lifelong learning, an ongoing examination of curriculum and teaching methods should be established.

The school should seek to broaden the scope of its educational program beyond the confines of the campus.

The enrollment should be gradually reduced to a level consistent with financial and physical constraints and the school's goal of educational excellence.

Diversify membership on the school's board of trustees and its committees.

Broaden and strengthen the financial base of the school.

Create a master plan for campus development. In addition, begin planning immediately to meet the following urgent plant needs: theater/auditorium/activities building, new dining room/kitchen facilities, renovation of the lower school, space for middle school science, computer classroom.

Establish a formal process for annual review of this long-range plan to evaluate continuing progress and commitment to its goals.

Coeducational boarding school in New England

The school will remain committed to excellence in the education of the whole person in mind, body, and spirit

► By teaching of the highest standards in the classroom.

► By inspiring the joy of pursuing excellence and fulfilling one's potential both in and outside the classroom.

► By instilling strong moral character, by developing leadership, and by

70

fostering positive attitudes and behavior, particularly respect and compassion for one's fellow human beings.

▶ By promoting the development of a positive self-image through both individual accomplishment and contribution to community life.

The school will provide the highest possible quality of community life for its faculty and students and will be committed to developing a community instilling responsibility, trust, mutual respect, and concern for the needs of those inside and outside the school community.

The school will continue to offer an outstanding academic and nonacademic program.

▶ The curriculum will be college preparatory and always strive to provide a demanding academic challenge and promote intellectual curiosity. The program will promote high standards in the fundamentals of creative thinking, reasoning, articulating, and calculating as well as seek to be innovative in elective courses offered.

▶ Nonacademic programs will be spread among athletics, the arts, and extracurricular activities.

▶ The school will take advantage of its greatest natural resource, the sea, and its location where appropriate in its programs.

The school will maintain its traditional Christian values and concerns as an integral part of school life, while welcoming and respecting the religious convictions and beliefs of others and affirming a sense of pluralism within the school community.

The school will recruit a board of trustees who represent a broad range of relevant backgrounds and interests.

The school will seek, develop, and maintain an outstanding faculty that is highly qualified professionally and personally committed to boarding school life.

The school will recruit a high-quality student body with a broad range of interests, talents, and abilities.

▶ To maintain the school's traditional character, intimacy, and coeducational balance, the school should not exceed x number of students.

▶ The school affirms its long-standing nondiscriminatory policy of admitting students of any race, color, or creed.

▶ The school desires a student body from diverse geographic, social, and economic backgrounds, enabling the school to be national and international in scope.

The school will maintain, upgrade, expand, and endow its physical facilities in order to support the mission of the school.

The school will continue to operate on a balanced budget and raise sufficient capital improvement and endowment funds in order to assure the school's financial future and to reduce gradually the school's dependence on tuition (and tuition increases) to meet current expenses.

The school will articulate clearly and project effectively its mission and make known its achievements—in academics, athletics, the arts, and extracurricular programs—to all its present constituencies and to colleges, donors, governments, and local communities, and will reach out and identify new constituencies.

Coeducational secondary day school in the West

1. The school's essential mission, as stated above and as adopted by the board of trustees on [date], will continue to set the course of the school's future.

2. The school shall be a coeducational day school, enrolling a maximum of 650 students in grades 7-12.

3. The school will enroll and retain a student body of high academic and personal potential and of diverse backgrounds and experiences.

4. The school will offer programs to develop special skills that will help students become responsible, contributing, self-sufficient members of a changing society.

5. The school will promote excellence on the faculty and staff and still provide faculty compensation that is competitive with the best packages among this state's public and independent secondary schools.

6. The school's physical plant will be expanded and improved to meet the needs of the educational program.

7. The school will increase its associations with the outside community and develop mutually beneficial ways of sharing school resources.

8. The school will provide financial resources to carry out these policies.

Appendix G.
Implementation Plans

The following examples show how to get started on an operational plan. The results of study and recommendations then can be projected forward for one year, three years, five years, and beyond. A format for organizing specific implementation plans for each policy goal, such as the one shown at the end of this appendix, can be useful.

1. Sample *suggestions* for implementation plans to be included in a report to the board.

Policy goal. To ensure that the school's faculty and staff compensation policies rank the school at or near the top of a selective peer independent school list, at least on a par with area public schools and as competitive as possible with other white collar businesses and industries.

Suggestions for implementation include researching compensation (salary and benefits) plans of peer independent and public schools and determining criteria for business and industry compensation research. Compensation policies should also support the need to explore nonsalary programs, such as sabbaticals and other study-travel grants, opportunities for professional development, and programs to provide incentives for teachers to remain in classrooms.

2. Example of an *initial set* of implementation steps to achieve the same policy goal (developed subsequent to the board's approval of the report).

a. The Personnel Advisory Committee will research current salaries and their relation to peer independent school and area public school salaries, with a report to the board by October 198-.

Policy Goal: Faculty and Staff Compensation

Implementation

Action	Responsibility	Initiation date	Report date	Completion date	Resources needed	Approval authority	Overall appraisal
To research current salaries and their relation to peer independent and area public school salaries	_____ Committee	May 198-	Oct. 198-	Oct. 198-	Support from business office	Board	Year end
To secure the services of a local consultant	Head	May 198-	As necessary	Oct. 198-	Budget for fees not to exceed $X	Head/Board	Year end
To address current and potential non-salary programs	Faculty committee appointed by head	Aug. 198-	Nov. 198-	Nov. 198-	Support from other faculty, business office, others as needed	Head	Year end
	_____ Committee	May 198-	Dec. 198-	Dec. 198-		Board	

After the reports and recommendations to the board, examples of ongoing implementation might appear as follows.

Action	Responsibility	Initiation date	Report date	Completion date	Resources needed	Approval authority	Overall appraisal
To implement the new comprehensive compensation plan so approved	Head	March 198-	Semiannual	199-	Funding as approved by the board	Board	Annually
To raise an endowment of $X million to support the nonsalary compensation programs	Board Development Committee	Fall 198-	Monthly	Fall 199-	Budget of $X yearly, support of development office, services of fund-raising consultant	Board	Annually

b. The head, in consultation with the Executive Committee, will secure the services of a local consultant in salary administration by October 198-.

c. The Personnel Advisory Committee will include as part of its salary study a review of nonsalary benefits, with a report to the board by December 198-.

d. The Personnel Advisory Committee, after a thorough review of salaries and investigation of benefit plans, and the advice of the consultant, will make recommendations to the Finance Committee for changes in faculty and staff compensation by January 198-.

e. The Personnel Advisory Committee, in conjunction with the Finance Committee, will make recommendations to the board by February 198- for the achievement of the policy goal over a period of years.

Appendix H.
NAIS as a Resource

Among the services NAIS offers are statistical reports and publications, as follows.

Statistical reports
Each school must decide for itself what data are most pertinent for long-range planning. Too much information can obscure policy issues and be a burden to those in the school who are required to produce it. Too few data can impede informed policy decisions. Most of the data schools need are available within the school or locally. In addition, NAIS provides regional and national comparative data to schools in statistical reports each fall (tuitions and salaries) and spring (operations and enrollment).

NAIS also prepares, on request, special reports comparing selected schools in the areas of enrollments, tuitions, teachers' and administrators' salaries, operations income and expense, financial aid, and annual giving. For information about these reports, call the NAIS office of information services: (617) 723-6900.

Publications
The following NAIS publications may also be useful in the planning process.

Administrative Forum (newsletter)
Business Management for Independent Schools
CASE/NAIS Advancement Resources Directory
Evaluating the Performance of Trustees and School Heads
Faculty Salary Systems in Independent Schools
A Legal Primer for Independent Schools
The Selection and Appointment of School Heads